D1237620

Conjunctions

by Katie Marsico

CHERRY LAKE PUBLISHING · ANN ARBOR, MICHIGAN

A note on the text: Certain words are highlighted as examples of conjunctions.

Bold, colorful words are vocabulary words and can be found in the glossary.

Published in the United States of America by Cherry Lake Publishing
Ann Arbor, Michigan
www.cherrylakepublishing.com

Content Adviser: Lori Helman, PhD, Associate Professor, Department of Curriculum & Instruction, University of Minnesota, Minneapolis, Minnesota

Photo Credits: Page 4, ©Rashevska Nataliia/Shutterstock, Inc.; page 5, ©ETIENjones/Shutterstock, Inc.; page 8, ©iStockphoto.com/craftvision; page 9, ©06photo/Shutterstock, Inc.; page 10, ©MANDY GODBEHEAR/Shutterstock, Inc.; page 12, ©David Gilder/Shutterstock, Inc.; page 14, ©iofoto/Shutterstock, Inc.; page 17, ©ZUMA Press, Inc./Alamy.; page 18, ©Vasil Vasilev/Shutterstock, Inc.; page 19, ©HLPhoto/Shutterstock, Inc.; page 21, ©Golden Pixels LLC/Shutterstock, Inc.

Library of Congress Cataloging-in-Publication Data
Marsico, Katie, 1980–
  Conjunctions / By Katie Marsico.
     pages cm. – (Language arts explorer junior)
  Includes bibliographical references and index.
  ISBN 978-1-62431-181-9 (lib. bdg.) – ISBN 978-1-62431-247-2 (e-book) – ISBN 978-1-62431-313-4 (pbk.)
  1. English language—Conjunctions—Juvenile literature. I. Title.

PE1345.M37 2013
428.2–dc23   2013007030

Cherry Lake Publishing would like to acknowledge the work of The Partnership for 21st Century Skills. Please visit www.p21.org for more information.

Printed in the United States of America
Corporate Graphics Inc.
July 2013
CLFA13

Table of Contents

CHAPTER ONE

A Proud and Excited Artist

Nancy was excited to show off her painting.

Nancy headed into the school gym with her dad and little brother, Mitch. She was both proud and excited. Her watercolor painting was in the art show.

"I know my painting is in here somewhere, though I am not sure exactly where," said Nancy.

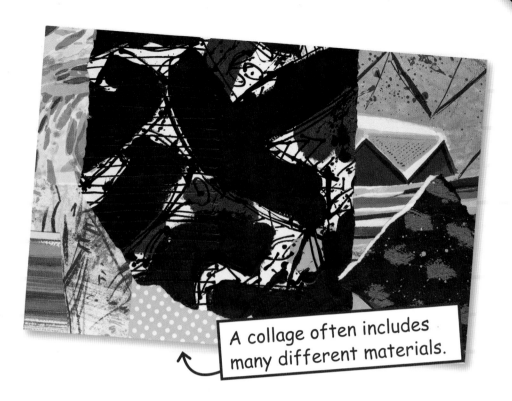

A collage often includes many different materials.

"Look, Dad," said Mitch. "There are sculptures, sketches, and photographs, too!"

"Of course," replied Nancy. "The kids in my class created not only paintings but also lots of other kinds of art. My friend Josh even made a collage out of things from his family's recycling bin!"

"We should get moving so we can check out all this amazing work," said Nancy's dad.

"Let's walk toward the back of the gym until we find Nancy's painting."

Conjunctions are joiners that link words, phrases, and clauses.

WORDS PHRASES CLAUSES

Nancy, Mitch, and their father used **conjunctions** to link their thoughts about the art show. Conjunctions are sometimes called joiners. They can join individual words together. Conjunctions can also join **phrases** and clauses. These are groups of words that have meaning but are part of a larger sentence.

People would find it hard to communicate without conjunctions. Sentences would be shorter, and language would sound choppy. If conjunctions did not exist, it would also be difficult to discuss complicated ideas.

ACTIVITY

Read and Rethink!

Read the following groups of sentences. Then connect the ideas in each group into one sentence. Use the conjunctions listed in parentheses. What differences do you notice after adding conjunctions?

1. Nancy liked drawing. She liked sculpting. She liked photography. (and)
2. Nancy enjoyed painting the most. This was why she decided to do a painting for the art show. (because)
3. Nancy had thought about using one of two types of paint. She had thought about using oil paint. She had thought about using watercolor paint, too. (either/or)

Answers may vary, but these are possible examples:
1. Nancy liked drawing, sculpting, and photography.
2. Nancy did a painting for the art show because she enjoyed painting the most.
3. Nancy had thought about using either oil paint or watercolor paint.

To get a copy of this activity, visit www.cherrylakepublishing.com/activities.

CHAPTER TWO

A Look at Conjunctions

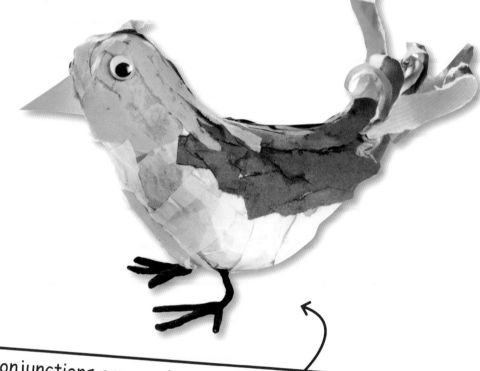

Conjunctions are used to connect ideas about several topics, including art.

"Hey, Gina," Nancy said to her friend. "I want to find my watercolor, but I would like to get a closer peek at your sculpture first. Did you use Play-Doh or modeling clay?"

"I made this with a mixture of water, flour, and newspaper," answered Gina. "It was messy yet fun!" The words *but*, *or*, *and*, and *yet* are conjunctions. With these joiners, no word, phrase, or clause is given more **emphasis** than another. The conjunctions *for* and *so* are also used this way.

For example, Gina used *and* to connect the words *water*, *flour*, and *newspaper*. She placed equal importance on each of the items.

A grocery list is one example of where people use the conjunction *and* to connect words.

Although Ethan took many photos, his favorites were of his family.

"If you like photography, then you should stop by my exhibit," called Nancy's friend Ethan.

"Wow, Ethan," said Nancy's dad. "When I saw these photos, I thought a professional had taken them!"

"I mainly snapped pictures of my family because they gave me my camera," explained Ethan.

Some clauses can stand alone as complete sentences. These are called **independent** clauses. Other clauses cannot stand alone. Instead, they depend on another clause to make sense. Certain conjunctions are used to connect such a clause to the rest of the sentence. The words *if*, *when*, and *because* are examples. There are several others, including *although*, *before*, *once*, *since*, *than*, *that*, *unless*, *where*, *whether*, and *while*.

For example, the clause "I mainly snapped pictures of my family," makes sense on its own. The clause "because they gave me my camera" does not. The conjunction *because* joins the two clauses together. It helps add information to the sentence. Now readers know why Ethan mainly took photos of his family.

"Either my art teacher forgot about my painting or it must be hidden somewhere," said Nancy sadly.

"Don't worry, Nancy," replied Mitch. "Dad and I would rather look for your watercolor all night than leave without seeing it!" Some conjunctions are paired together. *Either/or* and *rather/than* are examples. Others include *both/and*, *neither/nor*, and *not only/but also*. These conjunctions link words, phrases, and clauses that are of equal value within a sentence.

The conjunctions *either* and *or* are often used when choosing between two items.

Locate and List!

Locate and list the conjunctions in the following conversation:

"I love all this art, but the gym is so crowded," complained Nancy. "My art teacher should either find a bigger space next time or put the projects in three or four different rooms."

"Relax," said her dad. "I bet you will feel better once we find your painting!"

Answers: but, either/or, or, once

To get a copy of this activity, visit www.cherrylakepublishing.com/activities.

CHAPTER THREE

Recognize the Rules!

Make sure you use punctuation correctly when you write.

"Here are the watercolor paintings, but I do not see yours, Nancy," said her dad.

"Ooh, some people painted dinosaurs and robots," said Mitch excitedly. "Look! There are even watercolors of monsters, skyscrapers, and outer space!"

People follow certain rules when using conjunctions. For starters, most conjunctions fall between the words, phrases, or clauses they join together.

Punctuation is also important. If a conjunction links only two words or phrases, no comma is needed. For example, a comma does not separate *dinosaurs* and *robots*. Yet if a conjunction joins three or more words or phrases, commas are necessary. In the conversation on page 14, commas divide *monsters*, *skyscrapers*, and *outer space*.

The rule is different when joining clauses. Sometimes all the clauses are independent. These clauses would make sense as separate sentences. Then writers place a comma before the connecting conjunction.

Extra Example

Nancy was having a good time at the art show, but she was upset that she did not see her painting.

Independent clause #1: Nancy was having a good time at the art show
Independent clause #2: she was upset that she did not see her painting
Conjunction: but

What if one of the clauses doesn't make sense on its own? The punctuation depends on which clause comes first.

"I found my painting!" yelled Nancy. "I did not see it at first because of the huge crowd of people standing around it." In the last sentence, there is no comma before the conjunction *because*. No comma is needed when the independent clause comes first.

"Since your painting is so popular, I plan on displaying it in the coffee shop near my apartment," announced Nancy's teacher. In this case, the independent clause is "I plan on displaying it in the coffee shop near my apartment." It comes second in the sentence. The dependent clause and its conjunction are at the beginning. A comma is therefore necessary.

Nancy was proud because so many people liked her painting.

"Neither your brother nor I knew you were such a talented artist," said Nancy's father. "Either you should become a painter, or you should find a job doing some other form of art."

"Dad is right," added Mitch. "You deserve to win a medal or a trophy. Your painting is the best art here!"

Nancy's father used the conjunctions either and or to discuss her future as an artist.

Because Nancy named only two types of ice cream, there was no comma before the conjunction *and*.

"Now that you saw my watercolor, I vote that we go out for ice cream," said Nancy. "A scoop of chocolate and a scoop of vanilla are a good enough prize!" Conjunctions are not just important in conversations about art and ice cream. People use them all the time to link words, clauses, and phrases. Without conjunctions, language would be completely different. These parts of speech help people join ideas and information!

ACTIVITY

Read and Rethink!

Read the conversation below, and then rewrite it with the correct punctuation:

"Do you want to invite Gina Ethan and Josh for ice cream?" asked Nancy's dad.

"I would love to ask them but I think they need to pack up their art first," answered Nancy.

"It will take you a while to find your friends so I will help you look," offered Mitch. "It will be easier if you and I split up."

"We should decide on a meeting place," suggested Nancy's dad. "Once you gather everyone together wait by the front door."

To get a copy of this activity, visit www.cherrylakepublishing.com/activities.

Conjunctions make it easier for people to share their thoughts and ideas in speaking and writing.

Glossary

clauses (KLAWZ-iz) groups of words that contain a subject and a verb and form part of a sentence

conjunctions (kuhn-JUHNK-shuhnz) words that join words, phrases, or clauses together

emphasis (EM-fuh-sis) importance given to something

independent (in-duh-PEN-duhnt) able to stand alone

phrases (FRAY-ziz) groups of words that have meaning but do not form a sentence

punctuation (puhnk-choo-AY-shuhn) the use of periods, commas, and other marks to help make the meaning of written material clear

For More Information

BOOK

Fandel, Jennifer. *What Is a Conjunction?* North Mankato, MN: Capstone Press, 2013.

WEB SITE

BrainPOP—Conjunctions

www.brainpop.com/english/grammar/conjunctions/preview.weml

Watch a video that provides more information about conjunctions.

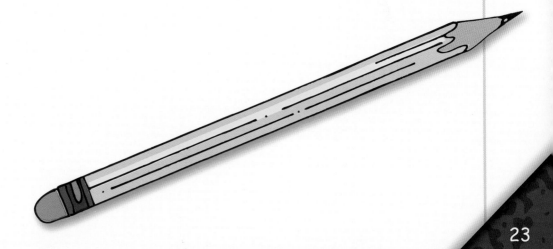

Index

About the Author

Katie Marsico is an author of children's and young-adult reference books. She lives outside of Chicago, Illinois, with her husband and children.